About this book

KW-235-723

This book has been carefully planned to help you become an expert. Look for the special pages to find the information you need. **RECOGNITION** pages, with a **yellow flash** in the top right-hand corner, contain all the essential information to know and remember. **PROJECT** pages, with a **grey border**, suggest some interesting ideas for things to do and make. At the end of the book there is a useful **REFERENCE SECTION**.

The fun of photography

Learning to use a camera

Everyone can enjoy photography — you don't have to be a professional to take a good picture. But to be an expert you will need to know more than just how to point the camera and press the shutter.

Understanding your camera
There are as many ways of taking a great photo as there are people with cameras. Some of the best photos ever taken were by people just enjoying their hobby. But all good photos have something in common: the photographer understood how the camera would see the scene in its mechanical eye before he took the picture.

This book will teach you how to do this. When you understand how your camera works you will double the fun of taking photos — and each photo is all the more likely to be a success.

TAKING PHOTOS

BY
Roger Vlitos

ILLUSTRATED BY
Dave Smith

MACDONALD

First published 1980

Macdonald Educational Ltd
Holywell House
Worship Street
London EC2A 2EN

©Macdonald Educational 1980
ISBN 0 356 06333X (paperback)
ISBN 0 356 063739 (hardback)

Printed by New Interlitho,
Milan, Italy

The camera imitates your eye

Every time you look at something, this is what happens: depending on how bright the scene is, your eye opens a tiny hole (the **iris**) to allow in the exact amount of light it needs. These rays of light shine a picture of the scene onto a spot at the back of your eye called the **retina**. There it is felt by the brain — and at that instant you are seeing.

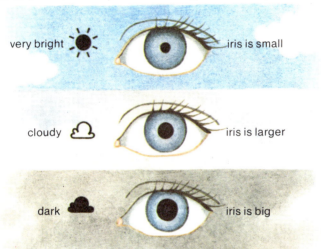

very bright — iris is small

cloudy — iris is larger

dark — iris is big

The size of your iris changes with the light

Your camera works in a very similar way. When you press the **shutter**, a tiny hole called the **aperture** is uncovered. This lets in just enough light to make an image on the light-sensitive film at the back of the camera. So the shutter and aperture on your camera work in the same way as the iris and the film is like the retina.

Funnily enough the pictures in both the eye and the camera are upside-down. The brain turns the eye's image right-side-up and to get a photo that is the right way round, the image on the film, called the **negative**, has to be transferred onto special photographic paper.

How a photo is made

All cameras have the same basic parts. You have seen how the shutter and aperture work. There is also a **lens** with which you can focus your picture to make it sharp, a **viewfinder** to look at the subject you are photographing and a **lever** for winding on your film.

A shadow print

A photograph is made by placing a negative on top of special light-sensitive paper in a dark room and then exposing it to light. The negative acts just like a stencil, blocking off light where it is dark and letting light through wherever it is pale. You can see how this works by making a shadow print with a leaf or piece of fern in a dark kitchen or bathroom.

Buy some plastic-based printing paper, such as Ilfaspeed or Veribrom, and three chemicals: **developer**, **stop bath** and **fixer**. You will also need three flat dishes, a towel to keep your hands dry and some photographic blotting paper.

The parts of a camera

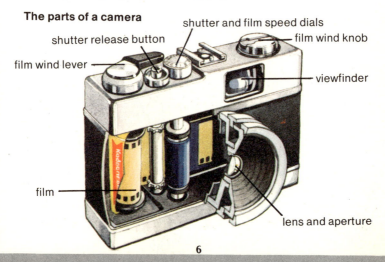

shutter and film speed dials

shutter release button

film wind knob

film wind lever

viewfinder

film

lens and aperture

1. Pour one chemical into each dish. Make sure the room is absolutely dark, then remove a sheet from the packet of paper. Place it shiny-side up under a lamp.

25 cm

2. Lay the fern on the paper. Then position the lamp about 25 cm above it. Switch on the lamp for **a split second only.**

blotting paper   fixer   stop bath   developer

3. Place the paper in the developer for at least a minute. Drop it into the stop bath for a few seconds, then transfer it to the fixer for one minute. Finally, rinse it under cold running water for at least two minutes to remove all the chemicals. Wipe off excess water with a pad of damp cotton wool then dry it between two sheets of photographic blotting paper. Rest a heavy book on top of the blotting paper to make your print dry flat.

The finished print

A pin·hole camera

The earliest type of camera was called a 'camera obscura'. It was just a dark room with a tiny hole in one side to allow light in. An upside-down image of the outside world formed on the wall opposite this hole, or aperture.

A pin-hole camera works in exactly the same way. Making one out of an old shoe box is one of the best ways of understanding how your camera works.

A pinhole camera

How to make one
Cut a flap in the lid of a shoe box so that you can look inside it easily. Then tape it firmly to the box.

Now make a small hole in the side and place a brightly-lit object in front of it. Make sure the room is dark enough — then look inside!

Using it as a camera

If you attached a piece of film to the back of your pinhole camera, placed a piece of moveable tape over the aperture to act as a shutter and then pointed it at a bright subject, it would, in theory, be possible to take a picture.

But photographs taken with a pinhole camera in this way are always rather shodowy and unclear — although experimenting with one can produce some interesting results.

Other difficulties

If you use your pinhole as a real camera you will have to load it in a dark room every time you take a picture. And as the aperture is so small, very little light is able to pass through it. This means that both the camera and the subject must remain completely still for several seconds in order to produce an image on the film.

So it is best just to use one to teach you the basic rules of how a camera works.

Experimenting with a magnifying glass

Using a magnifying glass

The reason that the image is faint at the back of your pinhole camera is because the aperture is so small. But if you were to make the hole larger you would get a blurred picture.

The way to avoid this is to place a lens in front of the aperture. Try this yourself by holding a magnifying glass in front of your pinhole. When the lens is held at a particular spot you will get a much sharper picture.

A camera lens

The lens is a very important part of your camera. Light has to enter the lens at exactly the right angle for the rays to meet on the film and produce a sharp image.

This angle depends on how far the lens is from the subject being photographed. If it is the correct distance away your photo will be sharp or **in focus**. But if it is too near or too far away, your picture will be blurred or **out of focus**.

9

Different kinds of camera

Now that you have read about how a camera works and how a photo is made, you are ready to start taking pictures. You may already own a camera, but if not have a look at the different types of cameras on these two pages and decide which is the best one for you.

If you are just starting, you will probably prefer an easily operated camera such as one of the pocket and Instamatic cameras illustrated below. More advanced cameras can be expensive — but keep your eyes open; you can often find a second-hand camera that is almost as good as new.

◄**Pocket camera**
Less expensive and easier to use than most cameras. Takes good photos as long as there is strong light and a still subject. Not as successful for close-ups.

▶ **Instamatic camera**
The most popular of all simple types. Easy to use with symbol controls for different light conditions, cartridge films and flash cubes. You can also buy a range of lenses to fit this camera.

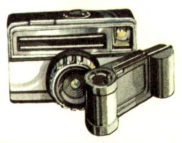

▲ **Subminiature camera**
Often called a 'spy' camera.

Full-sized enlargements can be made from the negatives.

◀ Direct vision camera

This camera has a viewfinder near the top through which you can see a miniature view of the scene which will be recorded by the camera. Some models also have a 'rangefinder' which indicates in the viewfinder when the subject is in focus. It will also take a range of lenses.

▶ Single lens reflex (SLR)

One of the most popular types of advanced camera because you see exactly the same image in the viewfinder as the one that falls on the film. A mirror reflects the image from the lens into the viewfinder. On these cameras you can change the size of the aperture and different lenses can be fitted.

◀ Twin lens reflex

Bulkier than the SLR because the lens, shutter and film are in the lower part of the camera with another lens, used for viewing and focusing, mounted on top. You can get sharper prints with this camera as the negatives are much larger.

▶ Instant picture camera

A package of chemicals develops the picture inside the camera within seconds. But the films are very expensive and the quality of the photos is not as good as those from the other cameras on this page. It has a direct viewfinder and uses bulbs or electronic flash.

Getting to know your camera

Every camera comes with an instruction booklet which you should study very carefully. Never load a new camera with film until you are sure you know exactly how to do it.

Start by taking outdoor pictures. If your camera has symbol settings for sunny or cloudy weather conditions, make sure you adjust it to the correct one. Then wind on the film until the first number shows in the little window. You are now ready to take your first photo. Good luck!

How to hold the camera
Always use your right hand for keeping the camera steady and for pressing the shutter.

This will leave your left hand free for focusing and making other adjustments.

Vary the position of your camera to suit your subject. You will probably find that you use position **1.** to take most of your pictures, but don't be afraid to turn the camera round to give a picture more length.

In position **2.** the weight of the camera should be supported by your right hand, while you focus with your left. Use your right thumb to press the shutter.

Remember, the smallest movement can cause a picture to blur, so practise holding your empty camera in these two positions until they become automatic.

The common mistakes

▶ Blurs and shakes
A camera only has to shake a tiny bit and your beautiful photo will turn out to be just a blur like this. So whenever you take a picture, keep absolutely still, hold your breath then slowly 'squeeze' the shutter.

◀ Bad camera angle
Can people walk up walls? Not unless they are Batman or are in a badly taken photograph. Always make sure that the image in your viewfinder makes sense before you click the shutter.

▶ Cutting off heads
If you are taking a picture of someone, one of the worst things you can do is to chop off their head! Keep looking through the viewfinder until the shutter clicks. Always think about what the camera's eye is seeing.

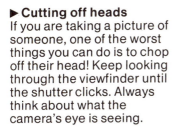

Which film?

The next question you should ask yourself is whether you want black and white or colour prints or whether you would prefer transparencies (slides). Your choice will depend on what it is you want to take as well as on whether or not you want to develop the film yourself. Developing colour films at home is a very complicated process — so buy black and white film until you become an expert.

Film speeds

All films are graded by their sensitivity to light or **speed**. Those which react to a very small amount of light are called **fast**. They are used when the shutter can only be open for a short time, such as when photographing a goal at a football match. A **slow** film gives much better detail — but it can only be used for long exposures. The speed of the film is printed on the box and is measured by the American Standards Association (ASA) or the German system (DIN). The higher the number the faster the film. Use a medium speed film for everyday purposes. (See the guide on page 59.)

Transparencies

A different sort of colour film gives transparencies or slides rather than prints. Instead of being turned into negatives the film is developed on a transparent base to match the colours originally photographed.

Slides look brighter and more natural than colour prints and they are also cheaper to process.

Slow black and white film
A slow film will give you good, clear details but any movement will tend to blur.

Look at the dramatic contrast between the sleeping woman on the grass and the moving dog in the foreground.

Fast colour film
A fast film is essential for all types of action photography — whether it's of a sports match or a flock of birds flying overhead.

As fast films react quickly, they are useful when the light is poor — such as in winter or on cloudy days. They can also be used for indoor photography.

Learn to be quick on the draw

It is easy enough to take a picture of a view or of someone standing still. But if you want to take action photos you must learn to develop a sense of timing.

Practice makes perfect
Carry your camera with you unloaded at first and practise your timing by clicking away at the things you see around you. Make sure that you are so used to the way your camera works that you don't have to think about what you are doing when you take a photo. Soon you will learn to recognize exactly the right moment to press the shutter — one of the secrets of an expert.

One of the best ways to practise timing is to capture dramatic scenes from your television set.

Shooting on sight

Always be on the look-out for things that happen suddenly and try to capture them on film. Be ready for any situation which may develop in front of you by having your camera adjusted to the proper settings and the film wound on.

The secret to being 'quick on the draw' is to be always prepared.

School sports days

Stand on the finishing line and get ready for the drama.

Always take two or three shots of each climax to be sure of getting a good one.

▲ Ready for action!

On holiday

Photographs are the best way of remembering all the fun you had on your holiday for years afterwards.

If someone in your family has a special hobby, try to take a few pictures of the most exciting or memorable moments for him.

If you are patient and have developed an instinct for 'the right moment,' you should be able to get some really dramatic shots.

Composition

Composition is the way you arrange things in your picture in order to make the most of your subject. A few seconds spent choosing the right viewpoint can make all the difference between a photo you will always treasure and one which you will quickly forget.

You should 'compose' your picture in just the same way as a musician composes a piece of music; each separate part should be there for a special reason. For example, a landscape will seem much larger if you take it with someone in the foreground.

Using your viewfinder
Whenever you want to take a picture, stand back and look for the best angle. Use your viewfinder as a frame and experiment with different approaches. Always try to find the best way to make the subject come alive.

Framing your subject

Telling a story

◄ A strong centre of interest

If you make your subject fill the viewfinder on your camera, it will give the picture more impact.

The cows in the picture on the left seem to be framed by the blurred leaves in the foreground. Because of this your eye is led towards the expression on the cows' faces.

Another good tip is to try and keep the centre of interest above the middle line of the photograph.

▲ Leading lines

Lines that lead your eye into a picture help to make it more interesting.

Notice how, in the picture above, your eye travels down the road and follows it into the distance.

The way in which the picture is composed makes us want to ask questions. Where does the road lead to? Is there anything behind the trees?

Try to make all your pictures tell a story like this one does.

The right exposure

'Exposure' means the amount of time it takes for a bright image to fall onto your film. The aperture controls the exact amount of light that the camera lets in and the shutter controls how long the light will enter for. A large aperture should be used with a fast shutter speed, while a slow speed makes up for a small aperture.

The speed of the film you use and the brightness of your subject will also affect your choice of exposure. A fast film will help you to take pictures in poor light, whereas a slow film might well give the best results on a bright sunny day.

negative

print

Under-exposed
This photo was taken with an aperture setting that allowed too little light to fall onto the film.

A negative that has been under-exposed will give you a print that has little or no detail in the shadowy areas.

Notice how dull the light parts of this print are.

Under-exposure is a common mistake, as people often don't realize how much light is needed to take a photo. You can buy a separate exposure meter to help you, or use a faster film.

negative

print

Correctly exposed
This picture was taken with the correct shutter speed and aperture size.

A correctly exposed negative will give you a print with both strong shadows and bright highlights.

This print is much easier to look at and understand than the other pictures on these two pages. The contrast between dark and light is not too harsh and there is far more detail in the middle tones of grey.

negative

print

Over-exposed
This negative shows very little detail because too much light was allowed to enter the camera.

The result is a print which is all contrast, with no grey tones in between. Again, try using an exposure meter — or a slower film.

More advanced cameras

The main difference between pocket and advanced cameras is in the amount of control the photographer has over what he takes.

The exposure guides on your camera are probably symbols like the ones illustrated on the opposite page. They do the same job as the **f numbers** on a more complicated camera. Each changes the aperture to suit the existing light conditions.

Aperture sizes or f numbers are arranged so that each is half the size of the one before it. The most common figures are: f2.8, 4, 5.6, 8, 11, 16, and 22. Remember, the bigger the number, the smaller the aperture size.

Use a shallow depth of field to make your subject stand out from its surroundings.

A large aperture size, such as f2.8, will blur a complicated foreground like this one.

Apertures

bright	cloudy	overcast
f 22	f 5.6	f 2.8

Most pocket cameras have a simple **fixed focus lens** which is designed to make everything from about 2 metres onwards equally clear. Advanced cameras have lenses which can be focused more sharply.

Depth of field

When you focus a lens on a particular object, a certain area in front of and behind it will also be in focus. The distance between the nearest and furthest objects which are in focus is called the **depth of field**.

By experimenting with your depth of field, you can take some unusual photos, like the one on the left. Here the photographer kept the foreground out of focus by concentrating on the middle-distance. This technique works especially well when you are photographing something through fencing or leaves.

Using a notebook

Always make notes when you take a photograph. Jot down the subject, lighting conditions, aperture setting and shutter speed (if your camera has one).

Then if you make a mistake you can check with your notes to see where you went wrong.

A really professional photographer can give this sort of information for every picture he takes.

How to make a dream sequence

A double-exposure is two photos on top of each other. Sometimes this can happen by mistake if you forget to wind on your film after taking a picture but most modern cameras have a special device to prevent you from exposing the same piece of film twice.

In some ways this is a pity because a double-exposure can make a very interesting photo, like the one on the right. Try making one yourself by projecting two slides together or by putting the whole film through the camera twice to make a dream sequence. (See below.)

A dream sequence
This works best in colour rather than black and white. You will need to use a cassette film like the one on the right. By putting it through your camera twice you can make a strange series of pictures that will look like something out of a dream.

1. Load the cassette film as you would normally, by placing it in the back of the camera and feeding the tongue of extra film onto the empty spool.

Close the back of the camera and wind on the film until the first number appears.

When making a dream sequence, the tongue of film is very important. You will need to keep it out of the cassette so as to wind on the film again later.

2. Now go outside and take a series of pictures. Remember that you are going to put two images together, so try to contrast the things you take on the first set of exposures with those on the second.

Why not make a background by taking pictures of water or trees or the pattern of the clouds in the sky?

3. When you have finished the film, wind it back carefully. Hold the camera to your ear and listen for the faint 'click' as the tongue of film slips off the right-hand spool.

Then open the back of the camera and feed the film onto the empty spool again. You are now ready to take your second set of pictures.

A double-exposure taken on a boat trip.

Portraits

A portrait is more than just a snapshot of a friend smiling at the camera. It should tell you something about that person and above all it should look natural.

There's no need to come very close to your subject; it will only make him feel awkward. Make people relax by chatting to them from behind the camera or by asking them to do something like playing with their dog or reading a book. Look for changes of mood and choose the moment which shows the person with a natural-looking expression.

Photograph people when they are not expecting it and you will get a far more natural-looking shot.

If you are photographing people who can't keep still, it is a good idea to take them against a background with an interesting pattern.

Then if they move you will still have a photo with a strong design, like the one made by the lines of the gate in the picture above.

If your subject is looking at the camera, always ask him to do something to break his pose. Take the picture as soon as he moves.

A hint of action will relax your subject and make the photo more interesting. Here the surroundings tell you something about the person.

Photographing animals

Animals make very difficult subjects — they always seem to move just when you want them to stay still!

Start by taking photos of your own or other people's pets. Make sure your camera is adjusted to the right settings then call your pet. As soon as you get its attention, press the shutter.

Wild animals

A fast film and a telephoto lens are useful aids when photographing wild animals. But success with birds or animals such as deer can often be due to good stalking. Always wear drab-coloured clothes, such as dark green and brown, keep the wind in your face so that your scent doesn't reach the subject and be careful not to make any sudden movements or you will frighten it away.

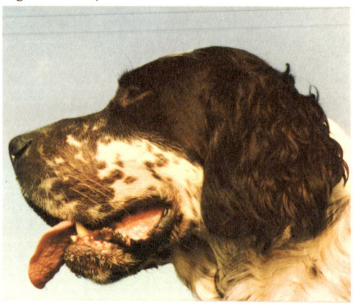

A portable hide

▲ Wildlife photographers often need expensive equipment to take good shots. But even if you haven't got a telephoto lens you can take good pictures from inside a portable hide. Make one yourself from pieces of sacking or dark coloured material — and then wait and see what comes along.

▼ Take close-up pictures of birds by hiding behind pot plants and photographing them feeding outside your windows.

Self-portraits

Taking a picture of yourself is not as easy as it sounds. Simply turning a camera round and pointing it at your head would produce a rather blurred photograph. But there are many other ways in which to take self-portraits and several technical gadgets available which will do the job for you.

Using reflections

Start by taking a picture of your reflection. You can use water, a mirror or a shiny surface like a metal shop-front or door. Focus on the surface and then pose yourself. If you shoot from the hip you can avoid having your face covered by the camera in the final photograph.

Now try taking a distorted picture of yourself. Photograph your reflection in a curved surface like a car's hub-cap, or a Christmas tree bauble, as in the picture below.

Using a delayed action device

Some cameras have a built-in delayed action device. This means that you can set your camera to click automatically after a few seconds.

It can be used for serious self-portraits, family groups or even for moments like the one above when you want to have fun with your friends.

A cable release

A cable release can also be used for self-portraits — although it is normally used to stop the camera shaking when you need a long exposure time. You simply focus the camera and then rest it on a level surface. Pressing the cable release plunger fires the shutter.

Picture ideas

Now that you have learned how to take photos of people, animals and even yourself, you are ready to move on to more unusual subjects.

The world around you

A good photographer can be like a painter. If you use your imagination, you can record unusual details of everyday life which are just as fascinating as a good painting. Look for the texture and pattern in the things around you. Whether you live in the town or country you should never run short of picture ideas.

▼ Using 'flare'
If you shoot into the sun, you may get patches of light or 'flare' on your picture.

These are caused by reflections off the surface of the lens. Here they add to the pattern made by the leaves.

►Texture and pattern

Using the right lighting is the key to adding texture to a photograph. It can show how something would feel if you could touch it.

Select a detail, like the sunflower head in the picture on the right, and take a close-up shot. Once you start looking at things more closely you will discover that even quite ordinary subjects can be made to look interesting.

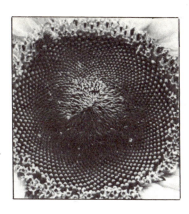

▼Looking at design

Details of buildings can also make interesting pictures.

Here the different shapes and patterns in the door make an unusual photo.

Lighting

A photo can never reproduce your subject; it can only record the light reflected from it. The word photography comes from the Greek words for 'light' and 'drawing'. This tells us how important light is to the camera — so always think about what the light is doing before you take your picture.

Choosing your light
Photographs are often judged by whether the light is interesting or not. If you screw up your eyes you will be able to see how the scene will look to the camera.

Are there any shadows? If there are none your subject may look rather flat and boring. On the other hand, sunlight shining directly onto your subject can produce shadows where they are not wanted — such as across a person's face.

The direction the light is coming from can also affect the look of your photo — as you will see from the pictures below.

▶ Lighting from different angles
You can make the same picture look very different by lighting it from different directions.

The first picture was shot with **front lighting**. Notice how it makes the bananas look flatter than they really are. The second photo shows how **back lighting** can be used to make a silhouette. **Side lighting** helps to show texture and gives the subject a more rounded effect.

1. Front lighting

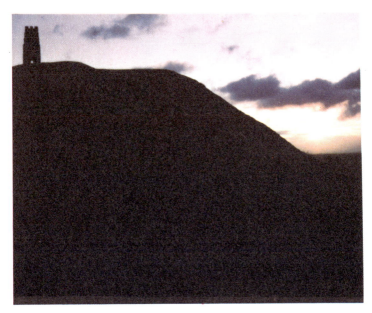

▲ Taking pictures into the sun can be tricky. Many films will slightly overexpose. But at dawn or dusk the light is much softer and you can take some beautiful photos.

In the picture above, the features of the landscape are dramatically silhouetted against the rich colours of the sky as dawn breaks on the first day of spring.

2. Back lighting

3. Side lighting

Taking photos indoors

Many photographers prefer to use studio lighting because they can create any light they choose instead of being dependent on the available light outside. However, the floodlights and spotlights used by professionals are expensive items of equipment. If you want to take photos indoors you can either use a very bright light bulb with a high speed film and a wide aperture, or you can use flash.

Which sort of flash?
Using a flash is much the easiest way of taking photos indoors and nearly all cameras can be fitted with a flash gun. You can either buy **bulbs**, which can only be used once, or an **electronic flash gun** which is more expensive but can be used for thousands of flashes. If you plan to take indoor pictures regularly, it is worth saving up for an electronic flash — a good one will last as long as your camera.

A flash can help pick up details which would be lost if you used only the available light indoors.

Notice how much more you can see of the subject in the photo above. Without flash, faces tend to go dark.

Lighting equipment

▲ flood light   ▼ spot light

The pictures above show examples of **flood** and **spot** lights. On the left is a picture of an **electronic flash** in an advanced camera and below it a **flash cube** with four bulbs attached to a pocket camera.

Flash extenders
You are bound to have seen colour photos that show people with bright red eyes. This is the reflection from the flash. You can prevent this from happening by buying an **extender** which will raise the level of your flash cubes.

flash extender

Using special films

Most films can be used in both natural and artificial light. But there are some colour films which are specially designed for artificial light and are worth buying if you plan to take a whole film indoors.

Ask your chemist or photographic dealer to recommend the best film for your type of camera.

Available light photography
Some indoor photographers prefer to work without any artificial light in order to make their pictures look more realistic.

This sort of photography works best in black and white. Use a **slow shutter speed** and a **wide aperture** with a fast film like 400 ASA and make sure your subject does not move too much.

Processing at home

When you have finished your film, you can either take it to the chemist for developing or you can do it yourself. The best way to learn is by joining a photographic club since film processing is a very complicated business.

Developing the latent image

Processing brings out the invisible, or **'latent'**, image on your film by changing it into a negative. The film is loaded into a light-sealed tank full of developing fluid. This chemical converts the film's emulsion to thin black silver wherever it was exposed to light. The film is then rinsed and 'fixed' by another chemical before being hung up to dry.

Monobath processing

1. It is possible to develop a black and white film in its own cassette by using a solution called **'monobath'**. This works best if you leave the first and last three frames of your film blank.

Simply cut off the tongue of film at the end then loop a few centimetres of the exposed film back around the cassette. Secure it with a rubber band.

2. Insert a **dowel rod** into the knob at the end of the cassette. Then slowly turn it anti-clockwise to loosen the film inside.

This will allow the monobath developer to spread over as much of the film as possible.

It is very important to do this properly. Otherwise you may find that your film has been developed unevenly.

3. Now lower the cassette into a container full of monobath solution.

Hold the cassette under with one hand and, with the other, use your wooden dowel to turn the film inside continuously during development.

Be careful not to rush things at this stage. Read the instructions on your packet of monobath and follow them carefully.

4. Break open the cassette and remove the film inside. Drop it straight into a bowl of cold water and run the tap over it for at least five minutes.

Monobath processing works in a different way from ordinary developing so there is no 'fixing' stage necessary. However, carefully washing off all the traces of the chemical will help you to get better prints.

5. Handle the negatives by attaching a clip to one end of the washed film. Treat them with great care at this stage — any fingerprints, scratches or specks of dust could ruin your final prints.

Wipe off excess water with clean fingers or a **very** soft sponge.

6. Weight the negatives with clothes pegs at the bottom and hang them up to dry.

Then cut them into strips of five or six and store them in protective cases until you are ready to print with them.

You can either use them to make contact-prints or for enlargements.

Developing contact prints

Not all your exposures will make successful photographs. You can save time and money by making small prints of your negatives at home and then deciding which ones you want to have enlarged. Contact-prints can be made in a makeshift darkroom like a bathroom or kitchen. You develop them in the same way as you did the shadow print on page 7.

A home darkroom

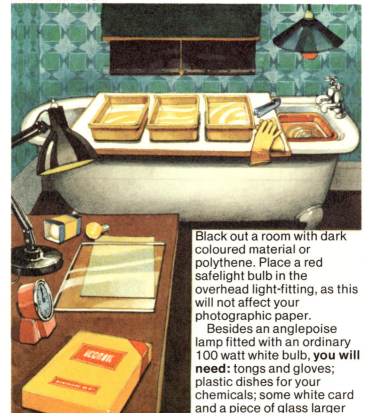

Black out a room with dark coloured material or polythene. Place a red safelight bulb in the overhead light-fitting, as this will not affect your photographic paper.

Besides an anglepoise lamp fitted with an ordinary 100 watt white bulb, **you will need:** tongs and gloves; plastic dishes for your chemicals; some white card and a piece of glass larger than your negatives; a clock and Grade 2 or 3 paper.

How to make contact prints out of your negatives

1. Check that your black-out material is properly in place, then switch on your safelight. Now turn on the lamp and make a note of the area covered by the light. When you have switched it off, remove a sheet of paper from the packet and place it shiny side up within this area.

Make sure that the clock is near to hand because you will need it in a few minutes to time your exposures.

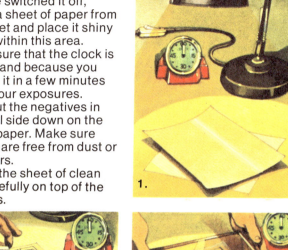

2. Lay out the negatives in rows, dull side down on the printing paper. Make sure that they are free from dust or loose hairs.

3. Place the sheet of clean glass carefully on top of the negatives.

2.

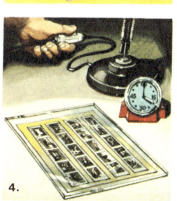

4.

3.

4. Now switch on the lamp for two seconds only. Turn off the lamp and cover a half the glass with your piece of card. Expose for two more seconds. These two different exposures will help you to decide on the best exposure time for your particular negatives.

Develop the paper in exactly the same way as you did when you made a shadow print.

Using an enlarger

When you made your contact prints you only reproduced images that were the same size as your negatives. But by using an enlarger you can make almost any size of print. Find out if there is one that you can learn to use at school.

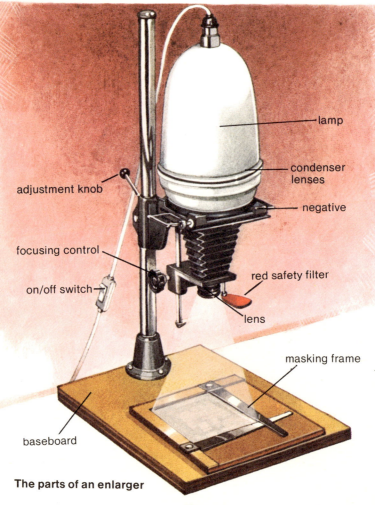

lamp

condenser lenses

negative

adjustment knob

focusing control

red safety filter

on/off switch

lens

masking frame

baseboard

The parts of an enlarger

How an enlarger works

An enlarger is very similar to a projector. The only difference is that instead of projecting an image onto a screen, the enlarger shines the negative's image down onto a piece of light-sensitive printing paper.

Enlarging is rather like taking a photograph. The negative, lit from behind, takes the place of the subject, and the printing paper acts like the film. An exposure is made, as on a camera, with the timing and the size of aperture adjusted to give the best results. The printing paper is then developed, just like the film in a camera.

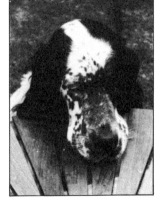

▲ 'Cropped' photo

Cropping

One of the most useful things about an enlarger is that instead of making the whole photograph bigger you can select just a small part of it for the final print.

This is simply done by raising the head of the enlarger.

In the photo on the left, the table and the pie take up most of the space.

But by lifting up the enlarger until only the dog's head covers the printing paper, we can **'crop'** the unwanted parts.

Notice how, when the photograph on the right was 'cropped', the dog's head became much larger.

Colouring by hand

The first coloured photographs were hand-tinted with inks. You can still see samples of this technique on old post-cards in junk shops. Of course hand-colouring will never look as real as a good colour print, but you can produce beautiful pictures this way.

Making a sepia print
Hand-colouring looks best on the golden sepia colour of old fashioned photographs. You can turn a black and white photo into a sepia print by using a **sepia-toning mixture** which you can buy from any photographic shop.

The method is very simple. A bleach in one tray takes the dark tones out of your print. Then, after you have removed and washed the print, you place it in another tray which contains the toner solution. Within seconds the picture reappears in a rich sepia colour.

1. Now moisten your sepia print with a ball of cotton wool. Use this instead of a brush to fill in the larger areas with different coloured paints or drawing inks.

2. Use a colour print if you have one and check your colours against it. Then fill in the details with a small brush. Build up layers of colour as the paints dry.

Finishing off

When the print is completely dry, you may like to mount it on a piece of card (as described on page 47).

You can make a hand-coloured print from any photograph but you will find that one printed on **matt** or **semi-matt** paper is much easier to paint.

If there is an old house in your neighbourhood like the one in the picture above, you might find it an interesting subject for a hand-tinted sepia print.

On the other hand, why not make one of your own house and give it to your parents as a present?

Displaying your prints

Having spent time, money and skill taking and developing your photos, it is worthwhile making the effort to keep them in good condition. The most important thing is to keep them free from dust and away from damp and direct sunlight. Most photograph albums will do this, but there are other ways in which to display your photos. Why not think up some ideas of your own?

Always remember to handle your prints with care and try not to get fingerprints on them. Hold them gently by the edges whenever you pick them up.

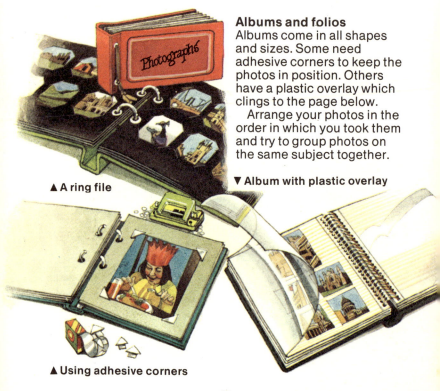

Albums and folios
Albums come in all shapes and sizes. Some need adhesive corners to keep the photos in position. Others have a plastic overlay which clings to the page below.

Arrange your photos in the order in which you took them and try to group photos on the same subject together.

▲ A ring file

▼ Album with plastic overlay

▲ Using adhesive corners

▶ Slip-in folders

These are usually for one photo only. You slip in a print which is then framed by a card wallet. This both displays and protects the photograph. You can buy these folders quite cheaply in either a stationers or a photographic shop.

▲ Scandinavian files

These are files made out of plastic sheets. Each sheet has a set of transparent pockets for your photos.

▶ Plastic cubes

These are ideal for displaying on a shelf or table in your room. They will take six pictures — one on each face.

◀ Mounting your prints

Mounting a photo on card is one of the most attractive ways of displaying it. Choose a coloured background to match the colours in the print. Black and white photos will look good against almost any colour.

Use double-sided sticky tape to attach the print to the card. But be careful not to press too hard or you may dent it.

How to use your pictures

A picture diary

It's all too easy to arrange your photos in an album and then put it away and forget about it. But using your photos to make a diary or storyboard can really make them come alive. Make one to record the life of your neighbourhood or your holiday.

Mount the photos side by side on a piece of card, using double-sided sticky tape. Try to arrange them so that each photo tells you something about the one than comes before and after it.

▼ **A picture diary of a holiday**

▶ Greetings cards

Mount photos on coloured card with glue or double-sided tape. Use your most artistic shots to make birthday or greetings cards. You can even photograph a Christmas tree or piles of presents to make some unusual Christmas cards.

◀ Framing your work

Search in junk shops for old picture frames that you can buy cheaply. Clean them up and then use them to frame your best photos.

A hand-coloured photo of a view or of your house will look especially effective like this and makes an unusual present.

▶ A calendar

Making a calendar from your prints is easier than it sounds. You will need 12 photographs — one for each month. Try to choose pictures that say something about each month. If your friend's birthday is in June for example, then use a picture of him for that month.

Mount the photos on pieces of thin card and then join them together. Ribbon or wool threaded through two holes at the top is a good way to do this.

Colour in the name of each month with felt-tips or drawing inks.

▲ A calendar of photos

Use the little pocket calendars that you can buy in any stationers to provide the dates at the bottom of each page.

Lenses and filters

Most cameras come with a fixed focus or **standard lens**. But you can change the lenses on many cameras to suit the type of picture you want to take. Check to see whether your instruction booklet says anything about this.

Filters are pieces of glass or plastic which can be fitted over your lens. They affect the way that certain colours are reproduced in your prints.

Standard lens
This will focus from 2 metres to infinity.

Wide-angle lens
This lens is able to 'see' much more of a scene — but the individual objects are smaller.

Telephoto lens
This allows you to select one detail and increase its size in your photo.

▲ **The same scene viewed through different lenses.**

It is difficult to take a photo in very bright sunlight.

Using a polarizing filter will help to absorb the glare.

◄ **Yellow filter**
Used in black and white photography. Good for landscapes as it darkens the sky in your picture so that the clouds show up more strongly.

► **Red filter**
This can make a blue sky look almost black so is especially effective when you are photographing a light object against the sky.

◄ **Ultra-violet filter**
You can leave this on your camera all the time to protect the lens from dirt and finger prints. It also cuts down haze and is useful for blue skies and seascapes.

Cheap tricks

Buying special photographic attachments can be an expensive way of taking more unusual photographs. But don't despair. If you are clever, you can make your own wide-angle or telephoto pictures by simply imitating what the real thing does.

One of the simplest tricks is to use sunglasses as a filter by holding them in front of your lens when you take a photo, as in the picture below.

▼ **A wide-angle panorama**

1. Take a series of photos from the same spot. Move the camera slightly to the right each time, making sure that the angle of view overlaps on each picture.

▲ Using binoculars
This trick works best with an
S.L.R. camera because then
you can see exactly what
your 'telephoto'picture is
going to look like.

Simply rest a pair of
binoculars on a solid base,
focus them on your subject
and then shoot through
them. The cormorants above
were taken like this.

2. When your prints are
developed, cut each one to
the same size.

Then fit them together and
glue them onto a piece of
thin card.

The camera can lie!

A toy hippo photographed through a macro-lens.

There is an old saying that the camera never lies, but there are at least a hundred ways to cheat the camera's eye! Remember the pictures you took for your dream sequence? They looked real even though they were double-exposed. Here are some other ideas for trick photographs. Use them to try and fool your friends.

Macro-lenses
These are specially designed for close-up shots. Use them to bring toys and models to life by photographing them against a realistic background. You can buy these lenses in metal mounts to fit most kinds of camera. Find out from your local photography shop whether yours can take one.

What is it?

Macro attachments can change the appearance of the most familiar objects. You can easily make your own 'what is it?' pictures like the one above.

Can you guess what this is a picture of? Turn the page upside-down to find out the answer.

The answer is . . . . . a toothbrush!

Using reflections

The picture above looks very realistic but of course it is only an illusion. The right-hand side of the girl's body is actually a reflection in the shop window.

Of course her other arm and leg are out of sight around the corner. If you keep your eyes open, you will find lots of opportunities for taking unusual pictures like this one.

Slide-showmanship

Putting on a slide-show is a great way to show people your pictures. But if you decide to have one, remember that the way you present your show is just as important as having good slides.

Preparing your slides

Sort out your slides before the show and discard any that are out of focus or too dark. Arrange them in the order in which you took them and decide on what you are going to say about each one.

A family slide show

Arranging the room

Make sure that the room you have chosen can be made dark enough for the slides to show up well. Position the screen before you start. The projector should be on a steady stand, level with the centre of the screen. Adjust the distance between them so that each slide fills the white area when it is projected.

Place a lamp near your boxes of slides so that you can find them easily. Finally, arrange the seating so that everyone will be comfortable and be able to see clearly. Always run through the presentation by yourself beforehand to make sure that the projector is in focus and that everything will go smoothly.

REFERENCE SECTION

Clubs and societies

One of the best ways to learn more about photography is to join a club at school or a local photography society.

Many clubs have special classes for beginners and learning can be a lot of fun with people of your own age.

Your local library should be able to give you a list of the clubs or societies in your neighbourhood.

The advantages of a club

Photography can be a very expensive hobby so it is best to start by using a club's darkroom until you decide whether or not you want to build your own.

Clubs offer you the chance to discuss your work with others and to receive free advice. Some of them also sell films and materials to their members at much cheaper prices.

Competitions

One of the best ways to improve your photographic skills is to enter a competition run by your local club or newspaper. Many professional photographers started by winning one of these. And even if you don't win, comparing your entries with the winning photos will teach you a great deal.

Buying film

The cheapest way to buy film is to go to a photographic shop and buy stock which is out of date.

All film has an expiry date marked on the side of the packet to warn people to use the film before its chemical coating starts to break down. After this date a film can no longer be relied on to give perfect quality.

But to protect themselves, manufacturers put the expiry date at least a month earlier than necessary. If you use it up quickly, it will be just as good as an ordinary full-price film.

Process paid films

These films work out cheaper than ordinary ones because you pay for the price of processing when you buy the film. When you have exposed the film you post it to the manufacturer for free processing into prints or transparencies.

Brand label films

Many large chemist shops sell their own brands of film at a cheaper price. These films are perfectly adequate for most kinds of camera — especially the Instamatic or pocket variety.

Film guide

Recommended black and white films

Speed	Brand	Quality
ASA 32	Kodak Pan X	Very fine grain on this slow film. Excellent for giant enlargements.
ASA 125	Kodak Plus X	Both have fine grain. The best b/w medium film for general subjects.
ASA 800	Ilford F.P.4.	
ASA 400	Kodak Tri X	Faster films with medium sized grains. Excellent for poor light conditions.
ASA 800	Ilford H.P.4.	
ASA 1250	Kodak Royal X Pan	Coarse grain. Suitable for Police surveillance work in very dim lighting.

Recommended colour films

Speed	Brand	Quality
ASA 25	Kodachrome II	Perfect for finer details but only available for 35mm cameras
ASA 64	Ektachrome X	Good daylight films for transparencies. Some difference in colour range between the two.
ASA 50	Agfachrome CT 18	
ASA 80	Kodacolour X	Daylight films for good colour prints.
ASA 80	Agfacolour CNS	
ASA 400	Kodacolour	Colour film for prints. Some colour quality lost due to film speed. Generally fast colour films are better for transparencies.

Glossary

Aperture: a circular opening which controls the amount of light entering the camera through the lens.

A.S.A: speed rating for films according to the American Standards Association.

Background: area behind the subject or the part of a photograph which is in focus.

Camera obscura: darkened room which was the forerunner of the modern camera. It was used by many artists through the centuries as an aid to drawing.

Contact frame: used to hold negatives flat in contact with paper when making contact prints.

Contact paper: specially coated paper of a very slow speed, used for making contact prints.

Darkroom: a light-proof room that is suitable for processing and printing photographs.

Depth of field: the distance in front of and behind the subject on which your camera can focus sharply.

Developer: chemical used in the processing of films and prints.

D.I.N: term used to rate film speeds according to the German Standards Organization.

Emulsion: the light-sensitive chemical coating on a film.

Enlargement: any print larger than the negative used to produce it.

Expiry date: date stamped on film packets to indicate the expected life of a film.

Exposure: the action of light on light-sensitive material to produce a picture.

Exposure meter: an instrument which measures the amount of reflected light from a subject, allowing you to work out the correct exposure.

F stops: numbers that tell you the aperture size. The higher the number, the smaller the aperture.

Fixed focus: a lens which is focused permanently on a distance from 2 metres to infinity.

Flare: reflected light from the surface of the lens which makes bright patches on a picture.

Flash: method of artificially lighting a subject for a brief moment in order to take a photograph.

Focusing: moving the lens closer to or further away from the film in order to obtain a sharper image.

Grade: types of photographic paper ranging from 0 − 5, indicating the degrees of hardness in the image produced.

Graininess: the texture of a photograph caused by dots which make up the image. Slow films have fine grain; fast films show large grain.

Lens: a circular piece of ground glass capable of bending rays of light.

Macro-lens: a lens which makes an image larger than the original subject.

Masking frame: used to hold different sizes of printing paper in position when making enlargements.

Latent image: the invisible image on a film or on paper after exposure and before development.

Negative: the reversed image of a photo produced after a film has been developed.

Positive: a print or transparency in which the light and dark areas are the same as the original subjects.

Retouching: improving a print which has blemishes.

Reversal film: used in making transparencies. The original film becomes the slide, by reversing the image from negative to positive in a chemical process.

Safelight: a darkroom light which will not affect the emulsion on photographic paper.

Slide: another name for a transparency.

Telephoto lens: a lens which enlarges the image of a subject a long distance away.

Transparency: the name for a positive image on transparent film.

Viewfinder: a simple lens designed to show you approximately what the camera is seeing.

Wide-angle lens: a lens which records a wider area of the subject than a standard lens.

Booklist

The Puffin Book of Photography by Christopher Wright (Puffin Books)

Pocket Guide to Practical Photography by John Hedgecoe (Mitchell Beazley)

Photographer's Handbook by John Hedgecoe (Ebury Press)

Basic Colour Photography by Andreas Feininger (Thames and Hudson)

Starting Photography by Michael Langford (Focal Press)

Photographing Nature by G.J.H. Moon (Reed)

Lighting for Photography by W. Narnberg (Focal Press)

The Camera by David Carey (Ladybird)

Magazines

These are the main general magazines in the UK:
You and Your Camera (weekly); *Amateur Photographer* (weekly); *Camera*, *Camera User* and *Photography* (all monthly).

Do's and Don'ts

Do keep the lens of your camera clean. Buy a packet of **lens cleaning tissues** from a photographic shop or chemist. Always breathe gently over the lens to moisten it before you wipe it with the tissue.

Don't use anything to clean your lens that will scratch or harm it in any way. Remember, the lens is the most important part of your camera.

Do put your camera strap around your neck or wrist when you take a picture. A dropped camera is easily broken and expensive to repair.

Don't load or unload your camera in bright light. Some films are so sensitive to light that you can lose up to three or four exposures like this.

Do check that your finger-tips, the camera case and stray bits of hair are all out of the way of the lens before you press the shuttter.

Don't handle darkroom chemicals without gloves on and keep them out of the way of small children in case they drink them.

Do study photographs and pictures you like and try to work out how they were taken.

Index

Acknowledgements
The photographs were taken by the author and **Sebastian Piper.**
Special thanks are due to **Fiona Anderson** for her help in the preparation of this book.